Methods
Of
Suicide

Sascha von Bornheim

ISBN: 146352109X
ISBN-13: 978-1463521097

LINKS

Shfpublishing.com

Facebook.com/shfpublishing

Facebook.com/officialsvb

Sascha von Bornheim

CONTENTS

ACKNOWLEDGMENTS

I'd like to thank the people who have encouraged me to write. Thank you.

Everyone else can fuck off.

Introduction

My first experience with suicide came at the age of 22, when I tried to leave the stage before the curtain fell. My plan involved 120 pills of Aspirin, and 20 sleeping pills. I had heard on TV that Aspirin acts as a blood thinner, which is why you shouldn't take it if you're out in the wilderness and have suffered a wound, as it will only make the bleeding worse. I thought that if I'd take enough of it, my blood would become so thin that my heart would have to beat faster and faster to keep pumping sufficient amounts of it through my body, eventually culminating in a fatal heart attack. But I wouldn't feel any pain, because of the sleeping pills. I mixed the Aspirin into a bottle of Coke, and proceeded to take large gulps from it with each sleeping pill.

As it turned out, I really did not feel a thing, but I awoke to an apartment that had vomit sticking to the walls, and my hair was soft and smelled a lot like shampoo. I have no memory of what happened after I ingested my little cocktail, but I evidently must have vomited out enough of the poison to remain alive, much to my initial dismay. A failure is a failure, after all; and those are never nice. For years afterwards I believed that my weak stomach was to blame for my lack of success, but then I read that only 1.8% of overdoses in the U.S. are actually fatal, since a lot of people –either consciously or unconsciously- vomit out whatever they had ingested… and that made me think: what if I had done some research beforehand? Would I still be here? Is there a better way to rid the world of one's own self?

I set out to find answers to these questions, and this book is the result of my investigations. Each of the methods that I examined is rated according to effectiveness in achieving death, and an explanation is given for said rating. My rating systems uses the + sign, with a maximum of 5 + signs for the most effective method, and no + signs for methods that have no hope of actually causing death. A 'Gore Rating' –pretty self-explanatory- is included as well.

I must strongly state that it is not my wish to either condone or condemn suicide; my only aim is to educate and to satisfy the curiosity of my readers. This book is for entertainment purposes only, and I assume no liability for any damages, injury, or death that may occur to anyone who has read this book.

You are responsible for your own behavior.

Cutting

Effectiveness Rating: + + + +

Gore Rating: Medium

Analysis:

This is a classic suicide method. I give it only 4+ because while it can be very effective, its practitioner must be willing to endure the pain of cutting into his own flesh. He must then wait until enough blood has drained from his body to cause hypovolemic shock, in which his body will at first try to compensate for the loss of blood. His heart will pump faster to keep up blood pressure, which, if the wounds are deep enough, will accelerate blood loss. Eventually, once the blood loss reaches 40%, the practitioner will feel extremely dizzy, and shortly afterwards, will lose consciousness. Hypovolemia, the state in which the volume of blood left in the system becomes too low to maintain vital functions, follows.

It is important that the initial cuts must be deep and target an artery, which carries fresh blood away from the heart, and thus has the highest pressure. This way one bleeds out faster.

The practitioner should ensure that he will not be discovered within an hour of placing the first cut, as bleeding out can take quite some time, depending on the size and placement of the wound. If one does not have the courage to cut deeply, then one should probably choose a different method. If that wasn't clear enough: if you're one of those retarded emo kids who pretends to be a Goth but you haven't actually got the guts to cut yourself, then don't. You'll just end up with really lame looking scars. Instead, continue dressing in green shirts and orange pants, and sooner or later you'll become the victim of a hate crime. This will then solve your problem of living in a world "with so much pain" while making the perps feel better about themselves for having rid the world of an emo kid. Everybody wins.

Jumping

Effectiveness Rating: + + +

Gore Rating: Medium to High

Analysis:

This is another classic method, but as you can see I have only rated it 3 + out of 5. There are two reasons for this: firstly, many jumpers choose places that are not sufficient in height to guarantee death; and secondly, survivors often suffer trauma to their bodies that may leave them paralyzed or otherwise impaired. In other words, they continue living, but their lives will be even worse than before their attempt, due to their newly acquired handicap.

I therefore cannot overstate the importance of finding a tall place to jump off of; a three story building will not guarantee a smooth transition into whichever afterlife the practitioner believes in. It is therefore recommended to spend some time scouting possible locations before committing oneself to an attempt that may end in quadriplegia. Kind of reminds me of carpentry: it's better to measure twice and to cut once than to measure once and end up in a wheelchair. Or something like that.

Guns

Effectiveness Rating: + + + +

Gore Rating: High to Extreme

Analysis:

Ah, guns. The easy way out… or so one would think. While it does not take nearly as much conviction to pull the trigger of a firearm as slitting one's own throat, guns are not exactly foolproof methods of killing oneself. Guns are popular in most countries as a relatively quick and thus painless way to escape form this plane of existence, but they do have their problems. Even with a gun inside the practitioner's mouth, the shot might not be fatal if the weapon is of small caliber or of a low-powered variety. A large caliber gun will cause significant damage to the brain and skull in general, but even then there is a small chance that the practitioner may live. Survivors are almost always left with scars or disabilities, some of which may cause chronic pain. Shots to the heart are also problematic, as the

practitioner must first know where exactly the heart is located, and then will have to hold the weapon at his own chest, at an odd angle, with a steady hand as he pulls the trigger. A second shot may be necessary to achieve the desired result. An extreme example: in February of 1995, an Australian fellow decided to end it all and shot himself with a shotgun. The pellets all exited through his back, without hitting a rib. He then shot himself in the head, from underneath his chin, but only succeeded in blowing half his face off. A third shot, aimed once again at his chest, finally destroyed his heart, and he, well, died.

The above example notwithstanding, what redeems the 'Guns' category is indeed the shotgun. A blow to the brain, from inside the mouth, delivered by a 12-gauge is practically guaranteed to be fatal in all cases, unless the practitioner has a tiny, tiny brain… which is why I'm rating 'Guns' as a category higher than 'Jumping'.

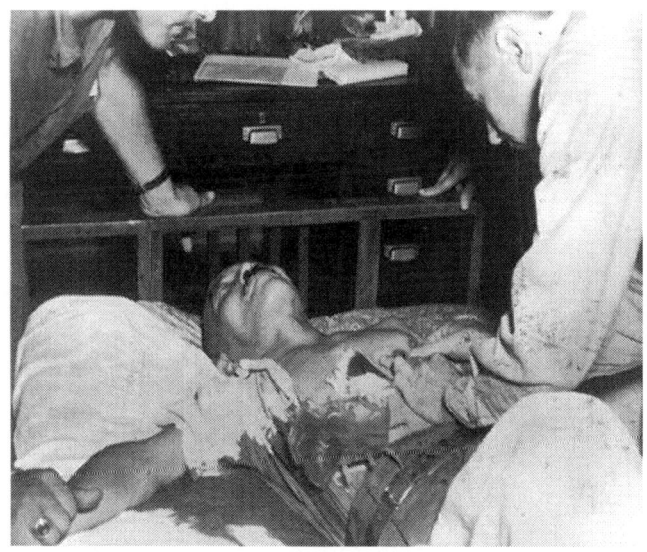

Japanese Prime Minister Hideki Tojo, who attempted suicide by shooting in 1945. He survived, but was hanged for war crimes in 1948.

Drowning

Effectiveness Rating: + + +

Gore Rating: Low

Analysis:

Drowning is another method that requires a certain will and conviction to carry out. Because drowning causes considerable pain and panic in the practitioner (due to lack of oxygen, and the struggle for air), it is a relatively rare method.

To facilitate drowning, the practitioner may use two devices; one, he may attach a weight to his body, thereby making it difficult or impossible for him to swim or even remain near the surface of the water; and two, he may choose a body of water that has strong currents, which he will be unable to fight. Brain death from a lack of oxygen usually occurs within 6 to 10 minutes, so it is important for the practitioner to make sure that there are no others (such as lifeguards) nearby who may save him during that time.

Unless the practitioner is simply an attention whore of course, in which case he purposely tries to fake-drown near a beach, in the hopes that Pamela Anderson will pull him from the water and perform mouth-to-mouth on him... only to discover that David Hasselhoff is the lifeguard on duty. A real suicide attempt then usually follows shortly thereafter.

Hanging

Effectiveness Rating: + + + +

Gore Rating: Low

<u>Analysis:</u>

Hanging has been around for a long time, and it appears to have remained popular throughout the ages. The reason is that almost anyone has the ability to do it; it is possible to hang oneself even from a doorknob, using a shoestring.

There can be two causes of death in a hanging suicide: suffocation, or the breaking of one's neck.

Suffocation occurs when the drop of the practitioner is not long enough (and thus does not carry sufficient energy) to break his neck. It is reported that the death of Nazi foreign minister Joachim von Ribbentrop at the Nuremberg trial took almost twenty minutes to occur after he had fallen through the trapdoors of the specially constructed gallows, because the hangman miscalculated the length of the rope. Even seasoned professionals make mistakes.

The breaking of the neck occurs when the rope is sufficiently long, and this will cause either paralysis (thus ultimately death through suffocation), or immediate death. On the other hand, you could simply be hanging there, totally paralyzed and unable to move, until you choke.

I rate it at 4 + because once the practitioner jumps off his chair (or his tree branch or whatever), it is very difficult for him to extricate himself from his position either way, which is why hanging has such a high success rate.

Conspirators in the assassination of Abraham Lincoln are hanged in 1865 in Washington, DC. This evidently isn't a suicide, but shows nonetheless how one would look after hanging oneself. Well, if one went to the trouble of renting period costumes before offing oneself in front of a large crowd, that is.

Auto-erotic Asphyxiation

Effectiveness Rating: + + + + +

Gore Rating: Low, but disgusting nonetheless

<u>Analysis:</u>

Auto-erotic asphyxiation is a fancy medical term for "jacking off while hanging yourself." It is accomplished exactly like a normal hanging, except that you would take your pants off at some point, and manage to live long enough after jumping off your chair or tree branch to begin masturbating. The practitioner would thus calculate the rope to be too short to kill himself instantly by breaking his neck; it would be short enough to strangle him slowly while he would be masturbating. The point of this is that apparently the lack of oxygen will give one a stronger orgasm... but why not simply hold your breath instead of hanging from the ceiling to achieve the effect? And think about the mess you leave behind... ew.

Electrocution

Effectiveness Rating: + +

Gore Rating: Low to Medium

<u>Analysis:</u>

Electrocution means touching live wires that carry at least 1A of current. In voltage terms, touching the wires in your house (110V – 230V, depending on where you live) is quite survivable, although not recommended if you want to live. Lightning strikes are also not nearly as fatal as some believe, as lightning has a tendency to travel over the surface of the body, rather than directly to the heart or the brain. It may however cause respiratory arrest.

A current as low as 100mA (a tenth of an ampere) can be fatal if it goes straight to the heart, by causing muscle spasms that either send the heart into disarray (with all the valves opening and closing out of sync), or disable it entirely (by freezing the heart muscles in a strong contraction). The practitioner would thus need to either find a source of strong, high voltage current, or he'd need to attach an electrode to his heart.

I find this method to be somewhat impractical, especially given that there is evidence that some victims of the U.S. electric chair need several shocks before they are declared dead (and this in a professionally "designed to kill" chair, not some home-made device), and some even catch on fire. I think I'd choose a different method myself; I'm not a huge fan of barbecued meat.

Suffocation

Effectiveness Rating: + + + +

Gore Rating: Low

<u>Analysis:</u>

The practitioner would pull a bag over his head, and seal it tightly. Death would then occur due to lack of oxygen, but there would evidently be a lot of struggling to breathe on the part of the practitioner, and since he is merely wearing a bag over his head, he can easily remove it.

It is however possible to fill this bag with a gas such as helium or nitrogen. This is usually done through a tube that is attached to a canister of some sort. An old gas mask from an army surplus store may also work, if suitable modified, and has the added benefit of allowing the practitioner to see the outside world through the goggles as the gas puts him to sleep. That would reduce the fear quite a bit, I think. Helium or nitrogen render the practitioner unconscious within 10 – 20 seconds, and death occurs shortly afterwards. For this reason I give "Suffocation" a 4 + rating, as it can be very effective and painless when planned properly. If you survive, you obviously didn't plan it properly. Idiot.

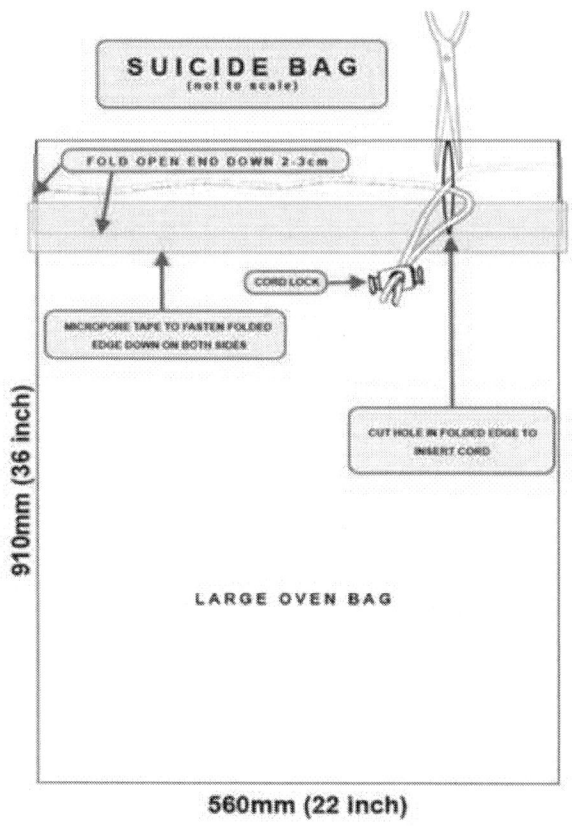

Diagram of a suicide bag, also known as an exit bag.

Trains

Effectiveness Rating: + + + +

Gore Rating: High

Analysis:

Jumping in front of an oncoming train will guarantee massive injuries, but does it guarantee death? It depends on where the train hits the practitioner, and at what speed. If he lies on the tracks then the train may actually simply pass over him, without doing any damage at all. He must therefore stand upright, with his head held slightly forward. It is important to note that the practitioner must never attempt this near a train station, as the trains are either slowing down to pick up passengers, or are accelerating away from the station. Either way, they are not traveling at a high speed, which obviously decreases the energy unleashed upon the practitioner when the train impacts his body. The same can be said for subway trains by the way: they are already decelerating when they reach a station, which makes any attempt pretty hopeless.

Thus, the practitioner must find a spot where the train is near or at its top speed, and that means on a long straight away. Of course, the train conductor may see the practitioner standing on the rails and attempt to brake the train, so it is wise to seek out cover (such as a tree or a bush) and hide behind it until the train is already close. Timing can be difficult, but a properly timed jump in front of a high-speed train has a great chance of being fatal. This may be a more viable method in countries that posses an extensive high-speed rail network than in countries where trains typically travel at slower speeds. In countries where the trains never actually come on time this method can be quite frustrating, so I would suggest that you travel to Japan to do this. First, they do have the famous Shinkansen high speed train; second, their trains are always on time, down to the half minute; and third, think about how many Japanese people you could piss off because your death on the tracks means that they'll have to wait until someone has cleaned your remains off the tracks until they can go work themselves to death in some factory. Also, you'd get to see Tokyo before you die... and if tentacle porn and talking robotic toilets can't make you change your mind about taking your life, nothing will.

As this method requires relatively little preparation and courage, I rate it 4 +.

Cars

Effectiveness Rating: + + +

Gore Rating: High

Analysis:

A suicide attempt by car is not very effective, in my opinion. As a pedestrian, who steps in front of a vehicle, the practitioner must obey the same rules as with the train method; that is, the car must be traveling at high speed and the driver must not have enough time to brake when he sees the practitioner. Even then, many modern cars are designed with pedestrian safety in mind, and feature crumple zones and space in between the hood and the top of the engine block, designed to protect pedestrians.

As a driver, the practitioner must keep in mind that especially modern cars are designed with occupant safety in mind, and the number of airbags installed in cars continues to increase. In addition, certain vehicles have the ability to notify emergency services through their telecommunications systems that an accident has occurred, and that help is needed. The vehicle then provides its coordinates to the rescuers via its own GPS system. Stupid modern safety technology.

Thus, an older car without such electronic wizardry is needed. Crashed at sufficiently high speed into a sufficiently immovable object (such as a bridge pillar), death can occur quite easily. The chance of grave injury, rather than death, is still great however; and the practitioner must remember that where there is a road, there are also other road users, who may call an ambulance upon witnessing an accident, or otherwise interfere with the practitioner's wishes. Seriously, people love nothing more than sticking their noses into someone else's business. Or entrails. That is why I am only rating "Cars" at 3 +.

Motorcycles

Effectiveness Rating: + + + + +

Gore Rating: High to Extreme

<u>Analysis:</u>

Everything I just said about suicide involving cars is also true about motorcycles.

There is however, one small difference between a car and a motorcycle: the motorcycle has no airbags. It also doesn't come with bumpers, or even seatbelts. And in some jurisdictions (particularly in North America), the rider isn't even required to wear a helmet. Add to that a power to weight ratio that is typically considerably better than any 4-wheeled device and the resulting machine is a death wish on wheels. That is why medical professionals sometimes refer to motorcyclists as 'organ donors', by the way. Thus, in general, motorbikes are a safer way to join the choir invisible than cars.

Airplanes

Effectiveness Rating: + + + + +

Gore Rating: High to Extreme

<u>Analysis:</u>

I am giving "Airplanes" a perfect score, because in addition to crashing at high velocity, they can also crash at high altitudes (on mountains), far away from civilization, which makes helping the pilot virtually impossible for the average human. They can also carry large quantities of aviation fuel, which may cause a fire or even explosion upon impact. And let's face it: planes get extra style points. They are impossibly cool.

The same caveat that applies to suicide attempts by car also applies to planes however: the practitioner must crash at sufficient speed to cause severe trauma or internal bleeding to die; otherwise he may just be injured and may be disabled for the rest of his life.

On the plus side, if he survives, he may apply to join his country's Special Olympics team!

Explosives

Effectiveness Rating: + + + +

Gore Rating: Extreme

Analysis:

This is an easy 4 + rating, in part due to the certainty of death occurring (as long as sufficient quantities of explosives are used), and in part because of the coolness factor of going out with a bang.

I cannot give it a perfect 5 + because of the inherent danger involved: unless the practitioner is an explosives expert he may injure himself gravely during the construction of his device. The device itself constitutes another problem, in many countries the sale and possession of materials related to making explosives is strictly controlled, and thus a certain amount of time, money, and patience is required to assemble all the necessary components. Such a suicide is thus not an impulsive one, but a well-planned and prepared one. This adds to the difficulty

of going through with the plan, but if one really wants
to go out with a bang… well, the results can usually
be seen on the front pages of local or even national
newspapers.

Poison

Effectiveness Rating: + to +++++, depending on poison used

Gore Rating: Low to Medium

<u>Analysis:</u>

Pesticides often employed in poorer countries, and in rural areas. The pesticides are available freely there, and in stark contrast to the "Explosives" category, these are often impulsive-driven suicides, without much prior preparation. Pesticide poisoning is a very unpleasant way to do the deed, as symptoms include respiratory problems, vomiting, diarrhea, cramps, convulsions, muscle twitching, and dizziness to the point of losing consciousness (which is probably a good thing; I wouldn't want to be awake while shitting myself).

So all in all, this is a pretty unsuitable method if the practitioner wants to go out with a bit of dignity, and it is quite painful. On the other hand, unless someone gets the practitioner to a hospital quickly, and he has swallowed enough poison, then death is virtually guaranteed, which earns "Pesticides" its second star. And it's pretty much the only way to go if you're really, *really* into masochism.

A more "civilized" way, if you will, is the use of cyanide. In small doses it will cause breathing difficulties and blurred vision, but in large enough doses it will kill within a few minutes (and after a few heart-stopping seizures). It is available in both gaseous and liquid forms, but may be difficult to procure. It has been used in suicide pacts (the people in Jonestown drank potassium cyanide laced Flavor Aid; and yes, Flavor Aid, not Kool Aid as is often reported), executions in the United States, and even comes highly recommended by Nazi war criminals wanting to escape the just punishment of being sentenced to death... by killing themselves. Retards.

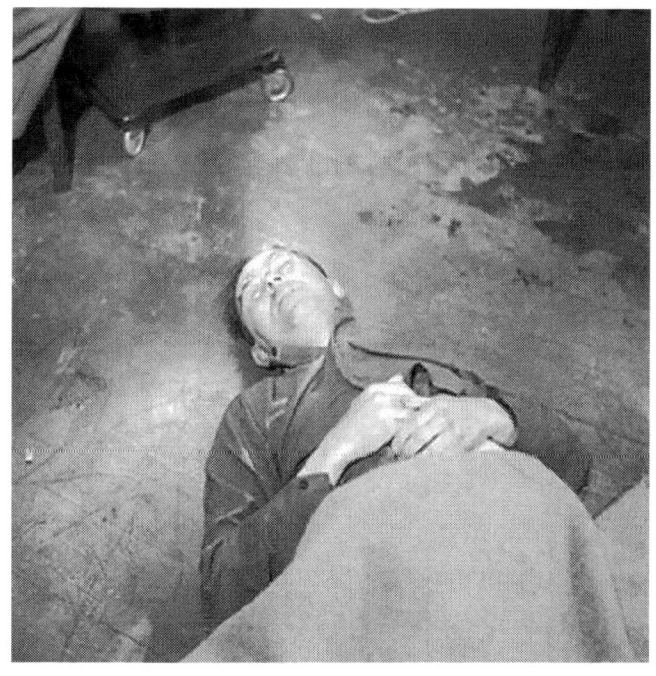

Heinrich Himmler, cyanide enthusiast.

Carbon Monoxide

Effectiveness Rating: + + +

Gore Rating: Low

Analysis:

Carbon monoxide poisoning used to be quite common. The practitioner would attach a hose to the exhaust pipe of his car, and then route the pipe into the car's interior. Death would result from the inhalation of the carbon monoxide in the car's exhaust gases.

Since the advent of the catalytic converter, this has become all but impossible. The catalytic converter removes around 99% of carbon monoxide from the exhaust gas, so attempting suicide in this manner is a waste of time and effort. Damn tree-hugging hippies with their save the planet catalytic converters!

All is not lost, however: a small oven or stove that burns coal may be the answer. If lit in an enclosed space, it will eventually produce enough carbon monoxide to fatally poison the practitioner.

It is possible to buy carbon monoxide detectors in many home hardware shops, as they are typically installed to warn the occupants of a house or apartment of high concentrations of the gas. This may be used by the practitioner to ascertain if the levels of carbon monoxide in his enclosed space are high enough to cause death in a reasonably short amount of time. An amount of 1600 parts per million (PPM) of carbon monoxide will cause nausea, convulsions and death within 2 hours. 3200ppm will cause death in less than half an hour.

This appears to me to be a relatively easy method of suicide, with little preparation involved for those who already have small coal-burning stoves or barbecues. If you haven't got one, then hanging may simply be easier.

Drugs

Effectiveness Rating: + (+ + + + + with qualified medical assistance)

Gore Rating: Low

Analysis:

As I have stated in my introduction, success with drug overdoses is thought to be only around 1.8% in the United States. In addition, certain barbiturates (pentobarbital, aka Nembutal) may be impossible to obtain in certain countries. In other countries, such as Mexico, Nembutal is still available from veterinarians. If taken orally, it is necessary to first ingest another drug that inhibits vomiting, as large doses of pentobarbital will make the practitioner throw up. The lethality of pentobarbital is quite certain by the way; the Chinese government uses it for lethal injections.

But many overdoses are actually a mixture of commonly available drugs and alcohol, or a mixture of illegal drugs and alcohol. The lethality of these is questionable, and they may leave the practitioner with severe organ damage or other health problems. This seems to be a rather ineffective way of killing oneself, and carries the risks associated with any sort of drugs experimentation. Using illegal drugs also means that the practitioner suffers the disgrace of going out like a hippie...

This is not recommended, unless the practitioner resides in a country such as Switzerland or the Netherlands where assisted suicide is carried out efficiently and safely by medical professionals trained in the use of legal drugs.

Has anyone ever invented a drug that isn't legal in the Netherlands?

Fire

Effectiveness Rating: +

Gore Rating: Low Gore Rating, but practitioner is covered in burn wounds; flesh or bones may be exposed.

Analysis:

Suicide by burning to death causes horrible pain to the practitioner, and if he is rescued before death occurs, he may be disfigured or otherwise disabled for the rest of his life. For these reasons, suicide by fire or "self-immolation" is relatively rare, although it has been used in the past by people who wanted to make a public statement, usually in protest of something.

Given the excruciating pain and the possibility of being rescued before the practitioner is well done, I cannot give "Fire" more than 1 +.

Starvation

Effectiveness Rating: +

Gore Rating: Low

Analysis:

Much like people who burn themselves, people who starve themselves to death often have a message to convey to the world. Starving takes a lot of conviction, as it is a long and slow death and it is by no means painless. It does have a high shock value (another similarity with "Fire"), but only occurs rarely in the western world. For the average man, it seems to be implausible to attempt, not only would the practitioner need mental strength and discipline for many days (even weeks) to carry out his plan, others in his proximity would likely find out about his activities and interfere with them. Eventually, the practitioner's tongue would swell and dry out to the point of cracking; he'd feel nauseous and drift in and out of consciousness... this seems like a needlessly complicated and painful way of dying, and much can happen to the practitioner and his convictions during the long period it actually takes to die. Thus, only 1 +.

Suicide Bomber

Effectiveness Rating: $+ + + / + + + +$

Gore Rating: Extreme

Analysis:

The suicide bomber is a hybrid of the "Explosives" and "Fire" types. On the one hand, he kills himself with explosives, but on the other hand does it in public, and tries to take some of the publi with him. He usually fights for a political cause, ar feels that this is the only way that he can get his message across. At the same time, he wants to avo the drawn-out pain and suffering of the "Fire" and "Hunger" methods.

As far as the actual use of explosives is concerned, I must give the "Suicide Bomber" all t advantages and disadvantages of the "Explosives" method. He is at risk of injuring or maiming hims unless he knows exactly what he is doing when he constructing his device.

I cannot, however, give him the same 4 + score that I gave the "explosives" method, because the suicide bomber usually kills innocent bystanders, and that is lame. Unless of course said bystanders aren't innocent at all, in which case the practitioner scores a 4+.

In a way though, the suicide bomber isn't really suicidal at all as he does not kill himself out of depression or desperation, but merely because someone in his religious/political organization told him to. And the "people who tell you so" never actually commit a suicide bombing themselves, preferring to live in luxury while their followers detonate themselves... you'd have to be pretty retarded to kill yourself for them, or for religion and politics, for that matter. So maybe it's good that such retarded people blow themselves up. One less idiot in the world, I don't have a problem with that. If all the idiots did that we'd be living in a happier world, although one supposes that the massive amounts of corpses and giblets from the millions and millions of assorted morons would begin to smell at some point, and then we'd have to get rid of them somehow, and god only knows what kind of a logistical nightmare that would be... dump them at sea, burn them, shoot them into outer space... ah well, we'll cross that bridge when we get to it.

Seppuku

Effectiveness Rating: $+ + + + +$

Gore Rating: Extreme

Analysis:

Seppuku is an ancient Japanese ritual in which a disgraced samurai cuts his belly open with a short sword. He would usually stab himself in the lower right belly area, and would then move the sword to the right. Then he would cut upwards, to the left again. This ritual would be performed in front of an audience, and the samurai would have an assistant, who would cut his head off after the samurai had performed his incisions. Well, he would almost cut his head off; the Japanese consider a head rolling around on the ground to be offensive, and thus the assistant would attempt to leave the head attached to the body by a small strip of skin.

Seppuku does not require an assistant; the practitioner will die from his wounds after a sufficient amount of blood has been lost. It is however excruciatingly painful, and thus the presence of an assistant is desirable. Whether that makes it then murder instead of a true suicide (the assistant murders the practitioner) is a difficult question.

One could argue that it is indeed a suicide, as the practitioner would have died anyway; but one could also say that the assistant killed the practitioner instead of helping him. The latter argument would of course ignore the fact that it is the assistant's designated and voluntary role to help the practitioner commit suicide, by relieving him of his pain. One could thus say that Japan was the first country in the world to allow assisted suicide… until they abolished the practice, in 1873. However, Seppuku is still sometimes practiced in Japan and even –very rarely- in Western countries. In spite of the obvious pain (or maybe because of it) I am giving "Seppuku" a 5 + rating. There is just something noble about willing to atone for your real or perceived dishonor by voluntarily going through that much pain. It's like giving the middle finger to the world and death simultaneously, while exclaiming, "I am better than you!" Respect.

Illustration of Seppuku from "Sketches of Japanese Manners and Customs", by J. M. W. Silver, illustrated by Native Drawings. Original published in 1867.

The End

There are many ways in which the practitioner can combine the different methods that I have described in the preceding pages. For instance, he could rig a bomb to explode in his car at the moment the car impacts with a bridge support at high speed. Or he could throw himself in front of a train after cutting his wrists. He could hang himself immediately after having taken a drug and alcohol cocktail. He could listen to a Celine Dion album until he feels the incontrollable urge to stab himself through the ears with a screwdriver, penetrating his brain and dying thusly to the sound of 'My Heart will go on… while my brain is thankfully already dead.'

There are no limits to human imagination and creativity, and I'm sure that we have yet to see the best (or worst) and most innovative way of leaving this world behind.

I'm gonna be watching the front pages of the newspapers…

***

If you are suffering from depression or other dark clouds in your life, there is only one real piece of advice that I can give you: it's never too late to die. Death is a door that's always open. But think hard before you walk through it, because there is no way back.

Take the time to think about your decisions and the impact they have, and take the time to talk to someone- anyone. A different perspective can make you walk through a different door, to discover things yet unseen. Why not risk living a little bit?

Thank you for reading this book, and if you have made it this far and are still alive, then please consider writing a review of it on amazon.

If on the other hand you are now about to kill yourself, then please buy another copy, it's not like you're gonna need your money anymore, right? Right.

About the author

Sascha von Bornheim was born in Germany in 1978. he currently resides in Canada, and writes both fiction and non-fiction. His first book, the autobiographical 'Journey to Freedom-Moroccan Stories' (ISBN 1451599080) was well received, and he is always working on a variety of different projects. Visit him at facebook.com/officialsvb

Sascha von Bornheim

7076422R00032

Printed in Great Britain
by Amazon.co.uk, Ltd.,
Marston Gate.